Jamestown
AMERICA'S FIRST PERMANENT ENGLISH SETTLEMENT

By Carole Marsh

Editor:
Janice Baker

Cover Design:
Michele Winkelman

Content Design:
Randolyn Friedlander

Gallopade is proud to be a member of these educational organizations and associations:

The National School Supply and Equipment Association (NSSEA)
National Association for Gifted Children (NAGC)
American Booksellers Association (ABA)
Museum Store Association (MSA)
Publishers Marketing Association (PMA)
International Reading Association (IRA)
Supporter of **Association of Partners for Public Lands (APPL)**

Published by
GALLOPADE™
INTERNATIONAL
800-536-2GET
www.gallopade.com

CAROLE MARSH BOOKS

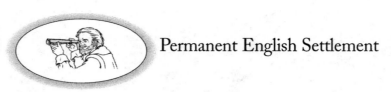

Other Carole Marsh Books

Orville & Wilbur Wright . . . Step Out Into The Sky!
Lewis & Clark Go On a Hike: The Story of the Corps of Discovery
"What A Deal!": The Louisiana Purchase
How Our Nation Was Born: The American Revolution
When Brother Fought Brother: The American Civil War
The Fight For Equality: The U.S. Civil Rights Movement
"It Can't Be Wrong!": The Bill of Rights
"Sign on the Dotted Line!": The U.S. Constitution
"Quit Bossing Us Around!": The Declaration of Independence
Jamestown: America's First Permanent English Settlement

State Stuff™, Available for all 50 states:

My First Pocket Guide
State My First Book
State Wheel of Fortune Gamebook
State Survivor Gamebook
State Illustrated Timelines
"Jography!": A Fun Run Through Our State

The State Coloring Book
The Big Reproducible Activity Book
State Millionaire Gamebook
State Project Books
Jeopardy: Answers & Questions About
Our State

Other Books in the Jamestown Series

The Mystery at Jamestown   Jamestown Trivia!
The Jamestown Storybook
Jamestown Readers

John Rolfe
Queen Anne
Christopher Newport
Thomas West, Lord De La Warr

Pocahontas
Chief Powhatan
Captain John Smith

Plus!
Historic Jamestown Mural

Table of Contents

Let's learn about Jamestown!

A Word From the Author

Dear Reader,

Every time I hear the story of Jamestown, I am amazed by the courage and determination of those first settlers in America! Can you even imagine what it was like to travel across the Atlantic Ocean for four or five months in a wooden sailing ship? Can you believe they were willing to start new lives in a complete wilderness where they had no idea what to expect? Don't you think it must have been hard to leave their families behind, realizing they would probably never see them again? It gives me goosebumps just thinking about it!

As you continue to study American history, you will see that our country was founded by very strong people! The story of Jamestown is a story of triumph and tragedy. The settlers were faced with disease, starvation, periods of conflict with the Virginia Indians, and days filled with extremely hard work just to survive. You know there had to be many days when they just wanted to give up and go back to their lives in England. But they stuck with it! Jamestown—the first permanent English settlement in North America—is the first example of the American spirit that makes our country great!

This book will introduce you to the people, the places, the events, and the issues of Jamestown. You will learn about the importance of leadership. You will see how geography influences lives in so many ways. You will realize that every community must have a way to make money and support itself. You will learn about life!

I hope you enjoy learning about Jamestown as much as I did writing this book. If we pay attention and learn from it, history is a wonderful teacher!

Carole Marsh

A Timeline of Events

🕐 **1570s**   Spanish missionaries begin a mission on the York River. Mission does not survive.

🕐 **1585**   Sir Walter Raleigh names the North American coast "Virginia."

🕐 **1587**   English settlers establish a colony on Roanoke Island. The colony was found abandoned in 1590. The colonists had vanished without a trace.

🕐 **1606**   Virginia Company receives a charter to start a colony in Virginia. Three ships set sail from England.

🕐 **1607**   The colonists arrive in Virginia and build a settlement on the James River. They name it Jamestown in honor of King James I.

🕐 **1607**   Colonial leader John Smith is taken prisoner by the Powhatan Indians. The chief's daughter, Pocahontas, asks that his life be spared.

🕐 **1608-9**   John Smith is elected president of the governing council. He returns to England after a gunpowder injury and never returns to Jamestown.

🕐 **1613**   The first sample of Virginia tobacco is sent to England.

🕐 **1614**   Pocahontas marries colonist John Rolfe. A period of peace begins between the colonists and the Powhatan Indians.

Jamestown:
America's First Permanent English Settlement

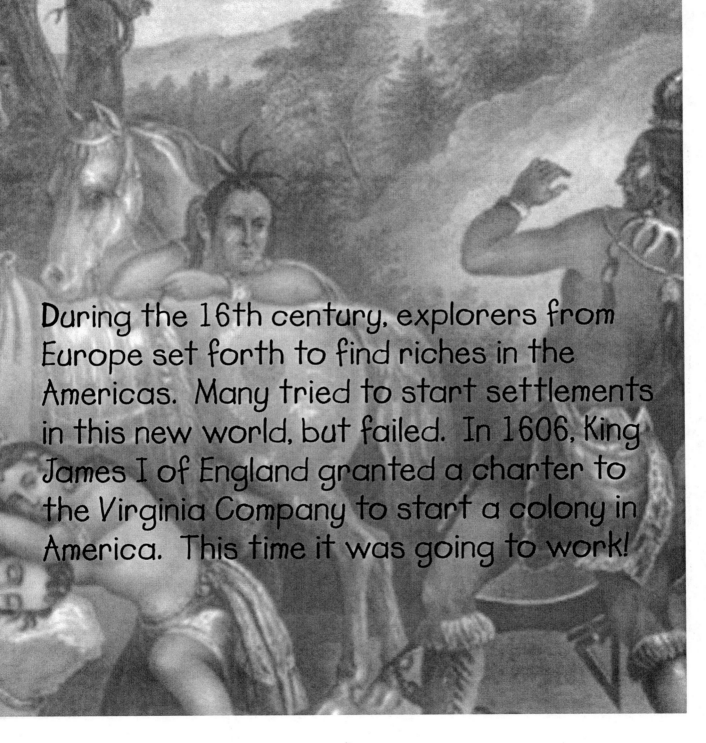

During the 16th century, explorers from Europe set forth to find riches in the Americas. Many tried to start settlements in this new world, but failed. In 1606, King James I of England granted a charter to the Virginia Company to start a colony in America. This time it was going to work!

In December of 1606, three ships set sail from London. They were named the *Susan Constant*, the *Godspeed*, and the *Discovery*. They carried just over 100 men and boys. After five long months at sea, the ships sailed up the Chesapeake Bay into a river. They named it the *James River*. On May 13, 1607, the colonists chose a spot to build their fort. They named it *Jamestown!*

Life was very hard in Jamestown. The settlers chose to settle where they felt safe from enemies, had a deep-water port, and had a good water supply. But the land was swampy and full of mosquitoes. Few of the colonists knew how to farm or live in the wilderness. They didn't have very much food, and many became sick and died.

Sometimes the local Virginia Indians were friendly and willing to help the colonists. At other times, they attacked the colonists. They even captured the colony's leader, Captain John Smith. They let him go after Chief Powhatan's daughter, Pocahontas, asked that his life be saved.

More settlers arrived in Jamestown in 1609, but the colony was almost wiped out in the terrible winter of 1609-10. The colonists called it "The Starving Time."

The few remaining colonists decided to go home to England. As they began their voyage home, two ships loaded with new colonists, a new governor, and supplies met them. The weary men agreed to stay and try again. Perhaps now things would get better ... it was worth another try!

The First Settlements

The Lost Colony

In 1587, a small group of people from England tried to establish a colony on what is now Roanoke Island in eastern North Carolina. Governor John White went back to England for supplies. When he returned in 1590, the colonists had all vanished. The only clue was the word CROATOAN carved in a tree.

The Jamestown Colony

In 1607, 105 colonists and 39 sailors set forth on three ships from London to America. One colonist died at sea. Five months later, the group arrived at the mouth of the James River. They named the settlement Jamestown.

Plymouth Colony

In 1620, a group known as Pilgrims sailed to America and founded the Plymouth Colony in present-day Massachusetts. They wanted to establish a colony with religious freedom. After a difficult winter, the Pilgrims celebrated the first Thanksgiving in 1621.

Match each picture below with the correct event.

The Lost Colony _____

The Jamestown Colony _____

Plymouth Colony _____

A.

B. CROATOAN

C.

The first English child born in America was named Virginia Dare. She was born in the Roanoke Colony, and disappeared along with the other colonists!

10

Let's Live Right Here!

The English colonists sailed across the Atlantic Ocean to get to Virginia. When they arrived in 1607, they founded Jamestown on a narrow peninsula bordered by the James River.

Why did the English choose Jamestown's location? They had three good reasons:

- They could defend themselves in case they were attacked by the Spanish Navy.
- The water was deep enough for ships to come in and out.
- They believed they had a good supply of fresh water.

Using a red crayon, circle the area where the English settled in Virginia.
Using a yellow crayon, circle the river closest to the English settlement.
Using a blue crayon, circle the name of the ocean the colonists sailed across to get to America.

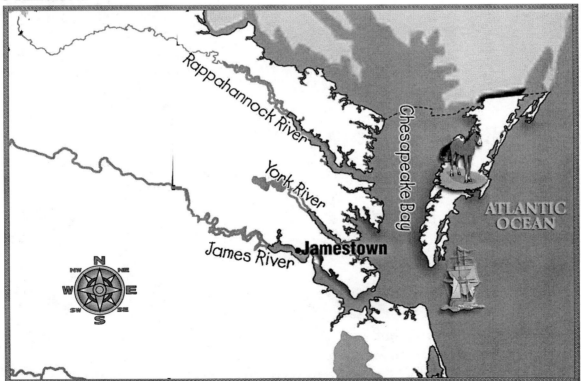

Bonus! Is Jamestown located in eastern or western Virginia? _____

Couldn't Make It Without Him!

The English colonists found life in Jamestown more difficult than they had expected. The site they chose to live on was marshy, and the drinking water was unsafe to drink. Many of the first settlers did not know how to hunt or farm. They had come to Virginia to earn a profit!

Captain John Smith was the leader of the colony. He saw that the colony would fail unless everyone worked. He made an important rule—"He that will not work, shall not eat." The people respected him and did what he said. Without his strong leadership, the colony of Jamestown may not have survived.

Circle the words below that describe a leader like Captain John Smith.

lazy

timid

good communicator

brave

sleepy

smart

foolish

makes decisions

silly

wise

organized

Solve the problem below to find out how old John Smith was when he reached Virginia.

12 + 6 − 10 + 11 + 3 − 5 + 10 = _____

You Go, Girl!

Pocahontas was the daughter of the powerful Paramount Chief Powhatan. When she was about 11 years old, the Powhatan Indians captured Captain John Smith. Captain Smith says that he was sentenced to death by Chief Powhatan, but Pocahontas begged that his life be spared. He was then set free, and began a friendship with Pocahontas.

According to Captain Smith, Pocahontas often visited Jamestown. She came with other Powhatan Indians as they brought food and furs to trade with the colonists. She sometimes brought messages from her father.

The name Pocahontas means "little mischievous one."

When Pocahontas was a teenager, relations between the Indians and colonists became tense. One of the colonists named Captain Argall kidnapped Pocahontas. She learned English and became a Christian. After she married a colonist named John Rolfe, there was a long period of peace between the colonists and the Indians. She is remembered as an important link between the Powhatan Indians and the Jamestown settlers!

Below is a list of ways to deal with conflict. Check those you think would have been good ways for the colonists to get along with the Powhatan Indians.

1. _____ Get together and talk about problems.

2. _____ Make fun of the Indians' customs.

3. _____ Organize a surprise attack.

4. _____ Use a person like Pocahontas as an interpreter.

5. _____ Be fair when trading goods.

6. _____ Thank the Indians for help with farming.

7. _____ Destroy the Indians' crops.

8. _____ Show Indians how to use tools brought from England.

WORD DEFINITION

Paramount chief: the highest-ranking Indian chief in an area

A Man with a Plan!

John Rolfe came to Jamestown in 1609, two years after the colony was founded. In 1612, John experimented with growing new varieties of tobacco in Virginia's fertile soil. He figured out how to "cure" the green leaves until they were brown. He shipped these dried leaves back to England in 1613, where many people wanted to buy them. John's tobacco crop was very successful and became the first crop to make money in Virginia. Tobacco allowed the Virginia colony to survive and thrive!

John's first wife died soon after he arrived in Virginia. He met Pocahontas a few years later when she was being held captive by the colonists. They were married in 1614. After their marriage, there was peace between the colonists and Indians for about eight years.

Put the following events in the correct order.

_____ John Rolfe marries Pocahontas.

_____ Dried tobacco leaves are shipped to England.

_____ Peace occurs between the colonists and Indians.

_____ John arrives in Jamestown.

_____ The Jamestown colony is founded.

_____ John experiments with growing tobacco.

_____ John learns how to dry the green tobacco leaves.

_____ Tobacco becomes the first crop to make money for the colonists.

Starting with Y, cross out every other letter to learn the name of Pocahontas and John Rolfe's son.

Y T P H B O R M Q A X S

— — — — — —

Master and Commander!

Captain Christopher Newport was a sea captain. He commanded the three ships that brought the first colonists to Jamestown. The ships were named the *Susan Constant*, the *Godspeed*, and the *Discovery*. Captain Newport sailed back and forth from England to Jamestown four more times. He brought much-needed supplies as well as new colonists. The colonists were lucky to have the support of a brave mariner like Christopher Newport!

Build a ship of your own!

Materials needed:
- 2 clean milk cartons
- 2 straws
- playdough
- long piece of string or yarn
- scissors
- glue and tape
- one popsicle stick
- brown and white construction paper

❶ Set the milk carton on its side. Cover the bottom half with brown paper (it may take two sheets).

❷ Cover the rest of the carton with white paper. Tape another piece of brown paper around the back of the carton. Leave one inch sticking up at the top, and go down 2 inches on either side.

❸ Roll two small hills of playdough and set them in the center of the ship.

❹ Cut the bottom section (3 inches up) off of the second milk carton. Turn the carton section so that the open part faces down and cover it with white paper. Tape the "ship deck" to the center of the ship directly over the playdough hills.

❺ Use a pencil to jab two holes into the deck right above each hill. Stick a straw "mast" through each hole into each hill.

❻ Cut a 3-inch square and a 4-inch square from white paper. Poke two holes in each and place these "sails" onto the masts.

❼ Cut a flag to glue at the top of one mast. Glue the popsicle stick straight out in front of the boat. Tie the string from the front mast to the stick. Decorate your boat with waves, a door, portholes, and whatever else you like!

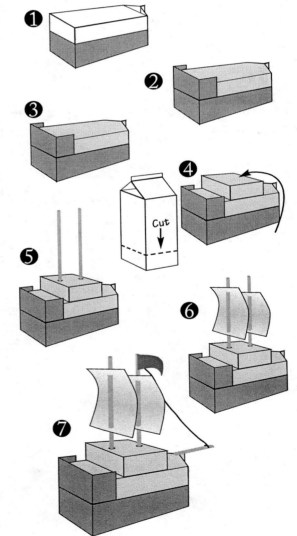

This Land is Our Land!

When the Jamestown colonists founded their colony in 1607, they had no idea how many Native Americans lived around them. Historians tell us that 13,000 to 14,000 Native Indians already lived in the area. Their settlements were centered around the rivers, which gave them fresh water, food, and transportation.

The Native Americans living in Virginia were part of the Powhatan Chiefdom. They spoke a form of Algonquian, a group of languages used by the Eastern Woodland Indians. Chief Powhatan ruled over more than 30 tribes. He was very powerful!

Although the Powhatan Indians were farmers, they were also warriors. They often battled with tribes in western Virginia over land, trade, and other issues. They were not pleased to see the English settlers move into Jamestown and continually take over their land. As a result, the Powhatans fought two great wars in 1622 and 1644 to drive the English out of Virginia.

Use the code below to find out the names of the two Indian reservations in Virginia today. The tribes are descendants of the Powhatan Chiefdom!

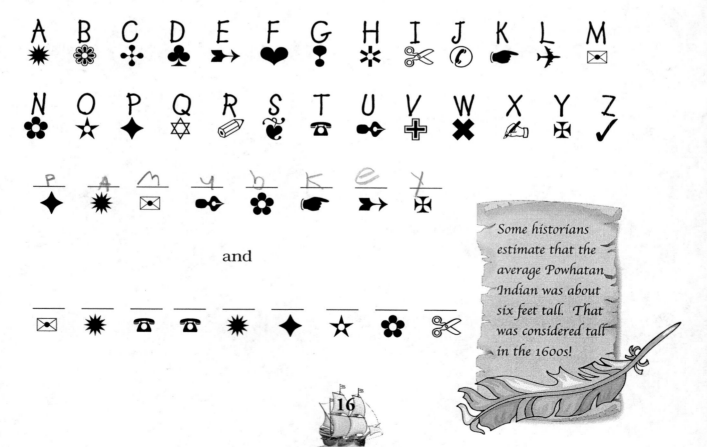

Some historians estimate that the average Powhatan Indian was about six feet tall. That was considered tall in the 1600s!

Daily Life as a Powhatan

The Powhatan Indians were farmers. They grew corn, squash, beans, pumpkins, and other vegetables. They also fished, hunted, and gathered nuts and berries. They called their house a "yehakin." It was a long house framed with wood and covered with matted reeds and bark.

Powhatan children entered adult life quickly. Girls married when they were about 12 years old, and boys married around age 14! Girls learned how to work in the fields and do household chores from their mothers. The older male tribe members taught the boys how to hunt and fish.

Make your own canoe like one that might have been used by Powhatan fishermen!

❶ Fold an 8.5x11" piece of paper (use any color) in half. Make a sharp crease.

❷ Make a 1/4" fold from the creased edge to one side, then fold it to the other side.

❸ Fold the open edges back to the 1/4" crease mark.

❹ Fold both edges up so the "W" shape is at the bottom and lay flat.

❺ Fold the corners up to about 1/2" from the top. Reverse the folds.

❻ Make a 1/4" fold from top edge that stops just above the corner fold. Make another 1/4" that folds over the corner fold. Repeat on the other side. Make all creases sharp.

❼ Use your fingers to push out the crease at the bottom of your canoe. This creates a hull and allows your canoe to float. Add the cut-out figure of the Powhatan fisherman.

Cut along the gray lines with scissors.

#4 side view

17

Welcome to James Fort!

The Virginia settlers built a fort soon after landing in Virginia. They knew they had to protect themselves from Virginia Indian attacks, animals, and other European armies. The fort was built in the shape of a triangle facing the James

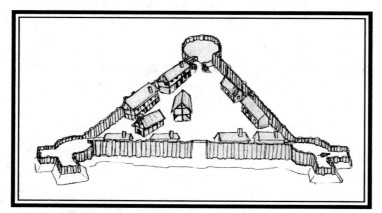

River. The walls were made of split wood poles and strong posts. Each corner had a raised area for a cannon.

Buildings inside the walls included a storehouse, church, and a guardhouse. The settlers lived in "mud and stud" houses made of wood and clay with thatched roofs. "Mud and stud" is a wall of sticks covered with mud and clay. About six to eight men lived in each house. Activities in the fort were centered around survival and finding something that would make a profit!

Read the list of activities below that may have taken place in and around James Fort. Write S next to each one that was important to the survival of the colonists.

1. ____ Gathering drinking water in buckets

2. ____ Fishing

3. ____ Making a fire for cooking

4. ____ Playing cards

5. ____ Hunting for deer

6. ____ Planting crops

7. ____ Gathering herbs for medicine

8. ____ Whittling a flute out of wood

9. ____ Telling stories around the fire

10. ____ Building houses

11. ____ Standing duty at the cannons and in the guardhouse

12. ____ Watching over the chickens and goats

Sassafras root was thought to be a powerful cure for fevers! It became a major export from Virginia in the 17th century. Today we use it to make root beer!

What Shall I Wear?

Clothing in the colonial era was handmade, expensive, and took a long time to make. Fashions did not change quickly like they do today, and clothing was even passed down through generations. Most clothing was worn out with use.

The Jamestown colonists wore practical clothing. Women wore long shirts called "shifts." They wore a short vest called a "bodice" over the shift. Women also wore several skirts but made sure they stayed out of the fire they were tending day and night. They also wore aprons and caps over their hair, and might even wear a straw hat in the sun.

Men wore shirts that came almost to their knees. They also wore a short coat called a "doublet," and short, baggy pants over long stockings. Most of the clothing was made of linen or wool.

Circle the things that you think a Jamestown colonist might wear.

a.

b.

c.

d.

e.

f.

g.

h.

19

Keeping Busy!

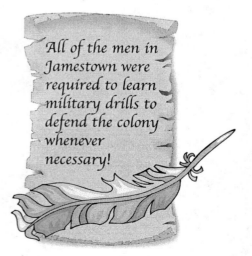

There were many jobs for people to do in Jamestown. Many of the first settlers were wealthy men (called "gentlemen") who were not used to hard work! Other settlers were craftsmen like carpenters and blacksmiths. Their skills were very important in building James Fort. The one doctor in Jamestown was also a very important person!

A large number of settlers were indentured servants. They were workers who had agreed to work for the Virginia Company for a specific number of years. In return, the Company paid their way to Jamestown and promised them a plot of land in the future. These indentured servants raised crops for food, as well as tobacco for sale back in England.

Match the Jamestown colonist to the comment he may have made.

_____ 1. "If I had all the tools I had in England, I could build one fine house!"

_____ 2. "Another working day to pay off my debt has gone by."

_____ 3. "We certainly needed that rain for the crops I planted today."

_____ 4. "I am not going to get my hands dirty by planting tobacco! I came here to search for riches in the New World!"

_____ 5. "I'm doing my best to make any tools the colonists need out of any metal I can find."

_____ 6. "I am exhausted at the end of each day taking care of these poor, sick people."

> A. farmer
>
> B. doctor
>
> C. carpenter
>
> D. blacksmith
>
> E. indentured servant
>
> F. gentleman

All of the men in Jamestown were required to learn military drills to defend the colony whenever necessary!

If I had a hammer...

I'd hammer in the morning!

The Dread of Disease

Disease took many lives in Jamestown. Most of the problems were caused by Jamestown's swampy location. The colonists used the salty water to drink, cook, and bathe. It became especially bad in the summer. One of the colonists described the water as "full of slime and filth." Mosquitoes bred in the water and carried germs in their bites!

The salty water caused salt poisoning, which the colonists referred to as "swellings." Many colonists died from two other diseases called dysentery and typhoid. Both diseases are usually caused by bacteria in water.

In addition, the colonists did not have a healthy, balanced diet. In fact, there was often very little food at all. They were very weak, and could not fight off disease when exposed to it.

Read each sentence below. Write T for True and F for False.

____ 1. Very few Jamestown colonists died from disease.

____ 2. The common cold caused many deaths in Jamestown.

____ 3. Jamestown's swampy location led to the disease problem.

____ 4. The colonists ate lots of healthy food.

____ 5. Salty water can lead to salt poisoning.

____ 6. Bacteria in water can lead to dysentery and typhoid.

____ 7. The colonists were often hungry.

Bonus! Can you think of one important thing you can do to avoid disease? See if you can fill in the blanks in the sentence below.

If you __ __ S __ your __ __ N __ __ before you eat, you can help avoid getting sick.

21

Finally—A Woman's Touch!

The first two women arrived in the Jamestown colony in October of 1608. Can you imagine the attention they got? Mistress Forrest came with her husband Thomas. Her maid Anne Burras quickly married a colonist before the end of the year!

Anne Burras was about 14 years old when she arrived in Jamestown! She and her husband John Laydon raised four daughters.

Other women came to Jamestown in the following years to become wives for the colonists. About 140 "maidens" arrived in 1620. They took care of the households, which included cooking, cleaning, gardening, and tending the animals (like chickens, pigs, and goats). Women made and mended clothes, and took care of the children.

Pretend you are a woman in Jamestown. Describe your day on the journal page below. Be descriptive! You might talk about the weather, or something funny that happened while doing your chores—be creative!

Date: _____

Name: _____

_____
_____
_____
_____
_____
_____
_____
_____
_____
_____
_____
_____

Say What?

Even though we speak the same language as the Jamestown settlers, things have changed over the years! Take a look at some examples of the "Queen's English" below!

The Queen's English

Hoigh *(for high) (pronounced as hoy)*: "There was a hoigh wind over the ocean."

Mought *(for might)*: "I mought go fishing today."

Recken *(for believe)*: "I recken we'll go to town on Saturday."

Salet *(for salad)*: "I'm going to cook up a mess of salet for dinner."

Toide *(for tide)*: "The toide is coming in and it's very hoigh!"

Smidgen *(for a bit)*: "Use just a smidgen of salt when you cook apple pie."

Tee-toncey *(for tiny)*: "I'll have just a tee-toncey piece of pie."

Chainy *(for china) (as in rainy)*: "She set out her best chainy for dinner."

Nary *(for not any)*: "He owns nary a thing but the clothes on his back."

Now it's your turn! Write some sentences of your own using the following words from the "Queen's English!" Don't forget proper punctuation.

Hoigh _____

_____

Mought _____

_____

Salet _____

_____

Smidgen _____

_____

23

The "Sot Weed" Saves the Colony!

The Virginia colony needed a way to make money to support itself. The colonists found it in a crop that grew well in the Virginia soil—tobacco! This crop saved the colony!

Tobacco was sold in England as a cash crop. This means that it was sold for money. By the time John Rolfe introduced it to Virginia, Europeans were already familiar with tobacco. It was very popular among the wealthy folks in England.

Just as today, not everyone was a big fan of tobacco. Some plantation owners planted tobacco instead of crops needed for food! Also, planters would take all the nutrients out of the soil by planting tobacco on the same land year after year. And, there were people who believed smoking tobacco was a bad thing to do.

Complete the dot-to-dot diagram below to see something used to smoke tobacco in the 17th century (and today, too!).

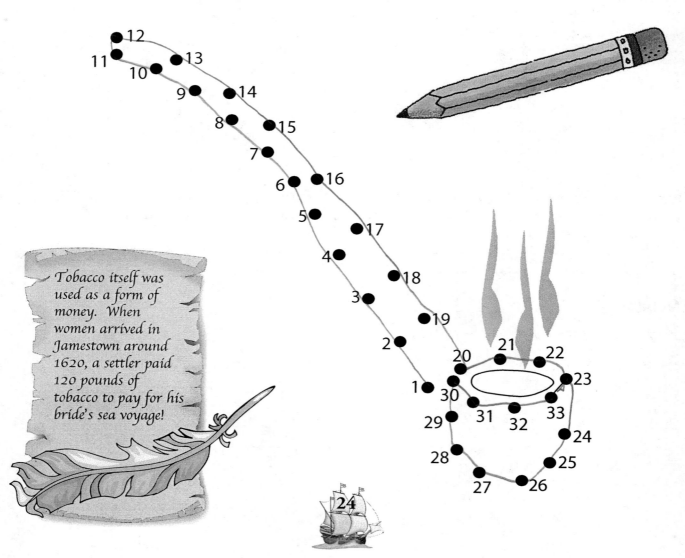

Tobacco itself was used as a form of money. When women arrived in Jamestown around 1620, a settler paid 120 pounds of tobacco to pay for his bride's sea voyage!

24

How Does Tobacco Grow?

Raising tobacco is no easy job! Seeds are planted in a seed bed and must be covered with a cloth for 8 to 12 weeks. Then the plants are replanted in a field, where the soil is continually worked to give it air and water. When the plants start to produce flowers, the upper part of the plants are cut off. This makes the leaves grow bigger.

When it's time for the harvest, the leaves are picked or the whole stalk is cut. The plants are placed on sticks and left in the field for a couple of days so they will wilt. The tobacco must then be cured (dried) in large barns built just for curing tobacco. Curing can take anywhere from a few days to several weeks. That's a lot of work, don't you think?

Draw some pictures! In each block below, draw a picture of a stage in the life of a tobacco plant!

1. seeds planted in a seed bed

2. farmer working the soil

The success of tobacco was astounding! In 1614, the colony shipped four barrels. In 1628, they shipped half a million pounds!

3. plant producing flowers

4. barn with tobacco plants curing inside

Africans Arrive

The first group of Africans arrived in Jamestown in 1619 on board a Dutch ship. The 20 Africans on board had been stolen from a Spanish ship. The Dutch exchanged the Africans for food!

Not all Africans in Virginia were slaves! Historical records tell us that many free Africans lived in Virginia. Most likely, they started out as indentured servants.

It is believed that Africans in Jamestown first worked as indentured servants, not slaves. But the success of tobacco changed the way the Africans were treated. More and more people were needed to grow and harvest the tobacco crop. Gradually, the length of service for Africans was increased. More and more Africans were brought to the colony against their will. If they tried to escape, they were forced to work for their master for the rest of their lives. By the middle of the 17th century, slavery was made legal in the colonies.

Using the word SLAVE, write a word or phrase that describes the life of African Americans in the Virginia colony. One of the letters is done for you.

S

_____

L

_____

A

_____

V

_____

E <u>scape was not allowed</u>

We're Out of Here!

The winter of 1609-1610 was known as "The Starving Time" in Jamestown. Bitterly cold weather and lack of food and supplies left only 60 people alive in the fort. The Powhatan Indians attacked the fort, preventing the colonists from getting to their food and firewood. When Sir Thomas Gates arrived in 1610, he was horrified by what he saw. He decided to pack up the survivors and head back to England.

Have you ever heard the saying, "Timing is everything?" In this case, perfect timing changed history! While sailing away from Jamestown, the survivors met an arriving supply ship from England. It was commanded by the new governor, Lord De La Warr. He convinced the survivors to turn back.

Thankfully, conditions improved in Jamestown under Lord De La Warr's rule. He was a strong leader!

The state of Delaware and Delaware Bay are named after Lord De La Warr!

Make your own compass with a few simple materials.
Materials: magnet, cork, large sewing needle, plastic cup filled with water

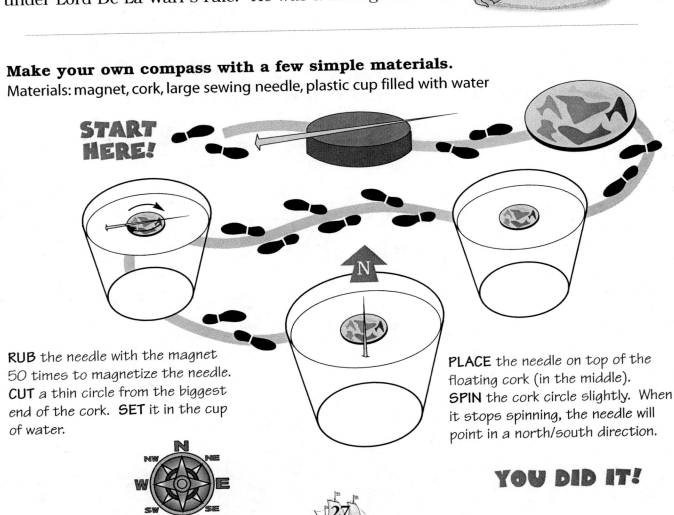

START HERE!

RUB the needle with the magnet 50 times to magnetize the needle. **CUT** a thin circle from the biggest end of the cork. **SET** it in the cup of water.

PLACE the needle on top of the floating cork (in the middle). **SPIN** the cork circle slightly. When it stops spinning, the needle will point in a north/south direction.

YOU DID IT!

# It's Time for a Government!

By 1619, Jamestown was becoming a stable community. Women had arrived and families were beginning to grow in the colony. Crops had been established to feed the settlers. Tobacco provided a cash crop so the colony could support itself. It was time for a new government to form!

The citizens of Jamestown formed a legislature in 1619. The General Assembly met in late July in the Jamestown church. There they elected the first English legislative body in North America! The assembly's job was to make laws for the colony, and serve as a court to hear any problems of the citizens.

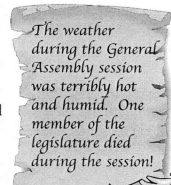

The weather during the General Assembly session was terribly hot and humid. One member of the legislature died during the session!

In their first six-day session, the legislature passed laws against drunkenness, laziness, and gambling. They also discussed protection against the Virginia Indians, and passed their first tax!

Answer the following questions.

1. Why do you think laziness was outlawed in the Jamestown colony?

_____

_____

_____

2. What were two jobs of the General Assembly?

_____

_____

_____

_____

Happy Anniversary!

The Jamestown colony celebrates its 400th anniversary in 2007! There are many interesting and exciting events planned during 2006 and 2007 to bring attention to the anniversary. Some of the special events are listed below!

A replica of the ship *Godspeed* (one of the three original ships that brought colonists to Jamestown) sailed to six major ports along the eastern United States. Those ports included Alexandria, Virginia; Baltimore, Maryland; Philadelphia, Pennsylvania; New York City, New York; Boston, Massachusetts; and Newport, Rhode Island.

The Jamestown Settlement living history complex will unveil a huge expansion in honor of the 400th anniversary. This complex includes replicas of the colonists' three ships.

Virginia Indian Heritage Events: Williamsburg and Hampton, Virginia

African American Imprint on America: Jamestown, Virginia

Journey up the James (the *Godspeed* sails up the James River): Chesapeake Bay and James River

World of 1607 exhibit: Williamsburg, Virginia

Opening of two new museums at Historic Jamestowne, highlighting the history of the 17th century settlement and the Jamestown Rediscovery Archaeology project.

America's Anniversary Weekend: Historic Jamestowne, Virginia

For details on all these events, visit this web site: americas400thanniversary.com

WORD DEFINITION

quadricentennial:
the 400th anniversary of an event

1607   2007

29

History Comes Alive!

Many historians used to think that James Fort had simply washed away into the James River. They were wrong! In 1994, archaeologists began to uncover the remains of James Fort. They were thrilled with what they found! Objects belonging to the colonists 400 years ago are now on display in a new museum called the Archaearium located in Historic Jamestowne. Over a million artifacts have been found!

Visitors to the Archaearium will see:

- helmets and breastplates
- weapons
- medical instruments
- personal objects like a child's leather shoe, buttons, and a man's ring
- coins
- tools like axes and a compass
- musical instruments
- pottery and dishes
- animal bones, fish bones, and other food remains

The Archaearium also uses computers to show how the fort would have looked on the land today. Visitors may also watch archaeologists excavating new finds! Do you think you would like to be an archaeologist?

WORD DEFINITION

archaeologist: person who studies ancient societies by looking at their buildings, tools, dishes, weapons, and other material goods

Glossary

anniversary: the date on which something happened in the past

artifact: an object made or used by people in the past

bacteria: living things with one cell that can be seen only with a microscope; some bacteria cause diseases

charter: an official paper in which certain rights are given by a government to a person or business

colony: a group of people who settle in a distant land but are still under the rule of their home country; or the place where these people settle

indentured servant: person committed to work for someone else for a fixed number of years

marsh: low land that is wet and soft; swamp

legislature: a group of people with the power to make and change laws

replica: an exact copy of something

respect: (verb) to have a high opinion of someone or something, or show that one has a high opinion of someone or something

Answer Key

Page 10
B, C, A

Page 11
Red = Jamestown, Yellow = James River,
Blue = Atlantic Ocean, Bonus = eastern

Page 12
smart, brave, organized, wise,
makes decisions, good communicator; 27

Page 13
1, 4, 5, 6, 8

Page 15
7, 5, 8, 2, 1, 3, 4, 6 Thomas

Page 16
Pamunkey, Mattaponi

Page 18
1, 2, 3, 5, 6, 7, 10, 11, 12

Page 19
D, E, F

Page 20
1.C, 2.E, 3.A, 4.F, 5.D, 6.B

Page 21
1.F, 2.F, 3.T, 4.F, 5.T, 6.T,
Bonus = WASH, HANDS

Index

Let's go check out the classified ads.

Good idea. I saw some lovely trees for rent the other day!